All
About
You
Journal

First Edition
3 5 7 9 10 8 6 4 2
FAC-025393-16074
Printed in China
ISBN 978-1-4847-8981-0

Visit www.DisneyBooks.com

THE Clementine
All About YOU Journal

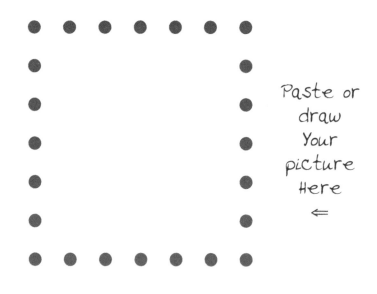

Paste or
draw
Your
picture
Here
⇐

This journal belongs exclusively to

....

This is me ⇑

SO—CLEMENTINE,
THIS MEANS YOU!—
IF YOU ARE NOT ME,
NO PEEKING, PLEASE!

This journal is about something you know everything about and are an expert on: YOU! It is a friend you can tell your secrets to, a place to be silly or sad, to write down every spectacularful idea that pops into your head, to share jokes, stories, feelings, and anything you want to say about you. Which means that there are no wrong answers, ever (I promise).

So make every page be just exactly the way you want it to be. You are the best you that ever was, and this is Y-O-U-R, YOUR JOURNAL!

from,
me
(Clementine)

You + You = You^2
(Me, Basically)

My Real Name: _____

My Secret Name: _____

My Name if I Was a Fruit: _____

I am this tall: _____

and wear size _____ shoes.

I really like my:

Teeth   Hair   Feet   Ears   Thumbs

Big Toes   Left Eye   Belly Button   Smile

(circle as many as you want and even make up your own.)

_____

_____

_____

_____

I was born on:

Month: ....

Day: ....

Year: ....

At this place: ....

....

Here is something I know about the
day I was born: ....

....

....

....

....

....

Here is what I looked like
when I was little:

The secret thing I know
about ideas is that once
they sproing into your head
you have to grab them fast,
or else they get bored
and bounce away.

My Best and Favorites

This is what I do best: _____

_____

_____

_____

_____

This was the best surprise ever: _____

_____

_____

_____

_____

_____

_____

When I was little, this was my favorite toy:

_____

_____

_____

Here is my favorite joke: _____

_____

_____

_____

_____

_____

_____

_____

_____

_____

This is my most favorite:

Color: ....

....

Game: ....

....

Book: ....

....

Book character: ....

....

TV Show: ....

....

Thing to eat: ....

....

....

My favorite trip
was when I went to:

_____

_____

This is why it was soooo great:

_____

_____

_____

_____

_____

_____

_____

_____

_____

_____

_____

_____

_____

_____

My dad says
if noticing interesting things
were a sport, I would have
a neckful of gold medals.

But I Do Not Like:
(Icks, Yucks, and Yipes)

What foods would be served at the awful-est meal you can possibly imagine?

_____

_____

_____

_____

_____

_____

_____

I can't eat eggs
if they have clear parts.

I always make a face
about doing dinner chores,
but the truth is I *like* being
in the steaming,
clattery jumble of
dinner-making
with everybody else.

What do you wish you never had to do
ever again?

What things scare you in a
hide-under-the-covers kind of way?

1.

2.

3.

CLEMENTINE'S LIST OF SCARY THINGS:

1. Ceiling snakes just waiting
   to drip on you.

2. Pointy things.

3. Boomerangs.

It's called

Throwing Someone Off the Track.

My parents say I am a genius at it.

_____

_____

_____

_____

_____

_____

_____

_____

_____

If I Could, I Would!

If I could be an animal, I would be a:

_____

Because: _____

_____

_____

If I could have any birthday present in the world, I would choose:

_____

Because: _____

_____

_____

_____

If I could be somebody else for just one day, I would be:

Because:

But then I would change back to being ME because I am so:

My stingray eyes
are extremely powerful.
I use them only in emergencies.

The Secret Me

Here are some things I secretly like:

1. _____

_____

2. _____

_____

3. _____

_____

Here's why I like these things to be secretful:

_____

_____

_____

_____

_____

_____

_____

_____

_____

_____

_____

_____

I felt my secret smile get
even bigger. It's a good thing I know
how to keep it from showing
on the outside.

Pizzazzy Talents

These are some things that I'm very good at:

1. ....

2. ....

3. ....

This is something I wish I was really good at, but maybe I'm not—at least not yet!

....

....

Maybe I had some really great talent I just didn't know about yet.

If I could get a trophy for one of my talents, it would look like this:

I am really good at math and drawing. But nobody gives out trophies for those things, which is unfair.

Waiting is
my hardest thing.

Your Family

Who is in your family? _____

_____

_____

_____

_____

What do you like best about your family?

_____

_____

_____

_____

_____

_____

If you could add somebody to your family, who would it be? ....

....

....

....

....

How come? ....

....

....

....

....

....

....

....

...in a family, there's always
an easy one and a hard one.
I guess it's a rule.

I am the easy one because: ....

....

....

....

....

But sometimes I'm the hard one because:

....

....

....

....

....

I had the proud feeling:
like the sun was rising
inside my chest.

Furry, Purr-y, Scaly, Finn-y, Hairy, Scary, and Imaginary!
(This Part Is All About Pets)

Are pets a part of your family? ....

If yes, what kind are they and what
are their names? ....

....

....

....

What do you love most about your pet?

....

....

....

If you don't have a pet, would you like to have one someday?

_____

Why or why not? _____

_____

_____

_____

_____

_____

_____

_____

What names would you choose for these types of pets?

A horse who smiles: _____

A cat who loves peanut butter: _____

A snake who might drop from the ceiling onto you: _____

A dog who sings: _____

A stinky hamster: _____

A super-smart parrot: _____

A space alien pet: _____

A funny pig who can fly: _____

I am expert at picking pet names.
I took the most beautiful word ever invented
for my kitten's name [Moisturizer!], but there are
plenty of good ones left.

Draw or paste a picture of
your real or imaginary pet here:

Since I got my kitten,
I'm not sure I really
want a gorilla anymore.
That would be a really big litter box.

Friend, Friends, Friendships

This is my newest friend: ....

....

I've known this friend the longest:

....

Ever since: ....

....

....

....

....

....

....

....

I'm like my friends in these ways:

1. ....

2. ....

3. ....

And different? ....

....

My hands smelled perfect:
a mixture of my new drawing pencils
and grape bubble gum.
It's hard to get your hands to
smell perfect like that. So I only
pretended to wash them.

Margaret washes her hands
one finger at a time.

I tried to shine with
valuableness.

Being Nicely Nice

I.O.U.s 4 U 2 MAKE

Here are some I.O.U. ideas:

1. I.O.U. 2 JOKES
2. I.O.U. 1 SETTING THE TABLE
3. I.O.U. 20 MINUTES OF LAUNDRY HELP
4. I.O.U. A FREE RIDE ON MY BIKE

I will make these I.O.U.s:

1. For:

   I.O.U.:

2. For:

   I.O.U.:

3. For:

   I.O.U.:

4. For:

   I.O.U.:

_____

_____

_____

_____

_____

_____

_____

_____

Imagine doing something
extra kind, like giving away
your ice-cream cone . . .

_____

_____

_____

_____

_____

_____

_____

_____

_____

_____

Life is *always* moving too fast

and we're *never* ready.

That's how life *is*.

But somehow that's just perfect.

H-A-Double-P-Y, Happy!

These things make me feel happy in an
I-Got-Two-Pieces-of-Cake kind of way:

1.

2.

3.

My happiest happy face looks like this:

A Small-ish Part About Being Sad

Who can always tell when you're sad?

....

....

When was the last time you felt sad?

....

....

What made you sad? ....

....

....

I scooped [my kitten] up
and he gave me a kiss on my ear.
"That's another way you are smart,"
I said. "You always know
when I'm sad."

What helped you feel better?

Sometimes you have to figure out
the problem before you can figure out
the solution.

When You Are M-A-D, MAD!!!!!!!!

What are some things, people, or stuff that happened that made you feel all hot and stompy?

_____

_____

_____

_____

Tell about a time when you were feeling a this-was-NOT-FAIR! kind of mad:

_____

_____

Excuse me, I am very mad about this journal. May I please have some Gummi Worms and a video?

Being Un-Mad

What (or who) makes you feel better when you are mad?

1. ....

2. ....

3. ....

4. ....

5. ....

6. ....

And suddenly it was a pretty good day in spite of the hole scrubbed into my head.

Feeling Better Quiz

Would these things change your
mad-bad-sad mood? (circle your best answer.)

1. A kitten hug?

    YES   NO   PURRFECT

2. Stirring grape jelly into your milk?

    YES   YUCK   YUMMY

3. Having a gorilla clean your room?

    YES   NO   I'M ALLERGIC

4. Feeling paid attention to?

    YES   NO   ALWAYS

5. Painting and gluing stuff?

    YES   NO   NOT SURE

6. Making someone laugh?

    YES   YES   DEFINITELY

7. Making a picture of the most un-boring thing you ever did?

> YES   NO   MAYBE

8. Writing what happened using ten different colors?

> YES   NO   LEMON-YELLOW

9. Squinching your eyes closed, spelling your whole name backward, and picturing a mountain of candy?

> YES   NO   IF IT'S GOOD

10. Twirling around and singing at the same time till you can hardly breathe?

> YES   NO   YIPPEE!

Just then, my father walked in. And suddenly, my nervous breakdown was over!

Style and Flair-to-Spare!

Would you wear a bowl on your head?
Socks on your ears? Make pants out of
grocery bags? Wear a shower curtain
cape? What would your craziest outfit
look like?

What does your favorite
I-am-being-fancy outfit look like?

WHAT'S ON TOP?

Take pictures or drawings of your face and add different hairdos or hats. You can draw these things or maybe find them in magazines, cut them out, paste them on, and— Hey, is that really you?

Now I did know
what it felt like
to have people clapping for me:
G-O-O-D, *good*.

Super-You!

What can you do in real life that's kind of super?

_____

_____

You can list your wish list of superhero qualities right here:

_____

_____

_____

_____

_____

_____

_____

Draw your superhero outfit!

WRITE YOUR SUPERHERO NAME HERE:

Superheroics

What would you do if you could become invisible?

_____

_____

_____

Would you rather be able to fly or have super strength?

_____

How come?

_____

_____

_____

_____

_____

_____

_____

_____

_____

_____

_____

_____

_____

_____

_____

I woke up with a superpower.
You can call me Magneto-Girl!

My parents are always going on
about the Golden Rule. "That 'Do' in
'Do unto others' can cover a lot of territory,"
they're always saying. My dad says
it could mean, "Be quiet in the movies,
as you would have others
be quiet in the movies unto you."

Room Enough for You?

These are the things I like best
about my room:

1. ....

....

....

2. ....

....

....

3. ....

....

....

My most fantastical bedroom would look like:

There is
no substitute for you.
You are one of a kind!

School Rules!

What's the name of your school?

_____

What grade are you in? _____

How do you get to school every day?

_____

Who is your teacher?

_____

Any favorite subjects?

_____

_____

Favorite way to spend recess?

_____

_____

_____

WHO'S WHO IN YOUR CLASS?

Major Goofball: ....

Scienciest: ....

Mathlete: ....

The Artsy One: ....

Actor/Actress: ....

Loudest: ....

Quietest: ....

Sports Star: ....

Very Fashionable: ....

Class Clown: ....

Most Daring-Will-Try-Anything: ....

The Question Asker: ....

Rule Your School

Fill in the blanks to make your own school rules!

I, Principal _____, now
that I am the Boss of Everyone
and In Charge of Everything,
do declare that these are
My Fun-tastic New Rules:

1. Classroom Rule: _____

_____

2. Recess Rule: _____

_____

3. Lunchtime Rule: _____

_____

4. Cafeteria Food Rule: _____

_____

5. Gym Class Rule: ....

....

6. Rule About Grades: ....

....

7. Field Trip Rules: ....

....

8. There will be no more: ....

....

10. And everyone gets to learn this in class:

....

....

....

Name four things (or more!) that you like
best about going to school:

1.

2.

3.

4.

(more).

Eating snacks helps us

when we're trying to learn things.

What's the hardest part of being in school?

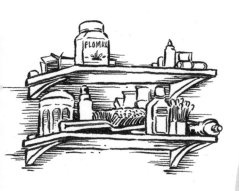

I have discovered
something—
the best names in the
world are on labels in
bathrooms.

Name Games

What is your fruit name?
(Think of a fruit that is a lot like you.)

_____

What is your favorite thing about your
real name?

_____

_____

If you had to pick a different name for
yourself, what would it be?

_____

How come? _____

_____

One way that I am like
my fruit name
is that I have
lots of sections.

Print each letter of either your real name or the name you would like to have on a separate line on the next page, and then write words or draw pictures of things that begin with that letter and that describe something about you. Like this:

C curious, creative, considerate, cat companion, complimenter

L letter writer, lizard liker, list maker

E elevator rider, enthusiastic, excellent (at drawing)

M mathematical, Massachusetts, Moisturizer (kitten)

E extravagant, enquirer, expert embellisher

N N-O-T not neat, noticer of interesting stuff, namer

T temporary tattoos, tool belts, talented

I I.O.U.s, imaginative, investigator, idea-comer-upper

N neighbor, nice, non-boring!

E extra kind, empathic, excited

Sometimes, on summer nights,

my family goes up to the rooftop. . . .

We bring up a large extra-cheese pizza

and a lamp with a really long extension cord,

and we all play the board game Life

up there on top of the city.

....

....

....

....

....

....

....

Your Perfectly Perfect Day

Imagine a day where everything is just exactly the way you want it to be. What would it be like?

_____

_____

_____

_____

_____

Tell about a real-life time where everything was just the way you wanted it to be:

....

....

....

....

....

....

June + July + August = Summer Days!

These are my top six favorite summertime things:

1. ....

2. ....

3. ....

4. ....

5. ....

6. ....

....

....

....

....

....

My dad does his research,
and he says *every* day
is some kind of holiday.

A Secret Letter

Do you like writing or getting letters? One of the great things about a journal is that it is PERSONAL and PRIVATE. Think about somebody that you would like to say something to, or ask a question about, or just let them know that you're thinking about them. It can be someone you know, someone imaginary or famous, your hero, somebody from a book or TV show, or a relative or pet. Write a secret "Dear Somebody" letter to tell that somebody something you've always wanted to say to or ask them.

Different Kinds of Lucky

I am lucky (in a most-of-the-time way) because:

1. ....

....

2. ....

....

3. ....

....

We sat there for a minute, breathing the bus air and thinking about who was lucky. "I guess we both are," Margaret said at last. "Just different kinds of lucky."

Goofy Goofiness

Are you ever a major goofball? What is
the goofiest thing you have ever done?

_____

_____

_____

_____

_____

What is the silliest thing you have ever
seen?

_____

_____

_____

_____

_____

What's your favorite joke? Or you can make one up right this very second.

_____

_____

_____

_____

_____

But this day
I saw something
even better
to do with my
itchy fingers!

Design Your Own
Tool-or-Other-Stuff Belt

If you think of tools as anything that
you can use or might need, you can dream
up all sorts of tool belts!

What would you put on these kinds of belts?

A making-a-sundae belt: ....

....

A very-long-car-trip belt: ....

....

A snowman-building belt: ....

....

It was the most beautiful
thing I'd ever seen in my whole
entire life . . . and if I wore it
I could build something
anytime I wanted.

Here is a secret good thing:
Sometimes I like journal writing . . .
because I can remind myself of things
I might forget when I'm a grown-up.

This, or That?

Pick just one silly thing from each of these choices. If you want, you can say why you like that one the most.

Would you rather:
Have an extra foot, or three ears?

_____

_____

Own a pet gorilla, or pet whale?

_____

_____

Shrink to the size of as a teeny bird, or grow as tall as a medium-sized mountain?

_____

_____

Live in a house made of clouds, or have a magical swimming pool in your backyard?

Wear a different hairdo every day, or never get to change it again?

Plant a cupcake tree, or a snack bush?

Be Hugely Famous, or a Secret Hero?

We'll all stay the same in some
ways, but we'll all change, too.
And it will feel crazy sometimes, and like
it's moving too fast. But it will be fine,
we'll adapt. Because this is how we roll.

Someday I Will . . .

When I grow up, I'll:

1. ....

2. ....

3. ....

4. ....

5. ....

6. ....

....

7. ....

....

My mother and father just looked at me as if I spoke in Martian, which I am going to learn.

Imagine that someday the President or a Very Famous Person is giving you an award.

This Extremely Important Award is being given to _____

for this Totally Amazing Thing:

_____

Draw your award here:

Congratulations!
Everyone in the Universe says "Thanks!"

AN ARTIST-DETECTIVE-MATHEMATICIAN

You might grow up to have more than one job, and maybe even more than one job at the same time. What cool job combos do you think you would like to have?

I WILL BE THIS, AND THIS, AND THIS:

1. _____ — —

2. _____ — —

3. _____ — —

4. _____ — —

5. _____ — —

6. _____ — —

Clementine says,

"I think it's a really good book."

Her dad says,

"I think it'll probably be a best seller."

_____

_____

_____

_____

_____

T-H-E E-N-D,
The End
This is the end of your journal.
Go ahead and add
"super-fantastic writer"
to your Pizzazzy Talents list!

Have you read these

Clementine

books?

Clementine

Clementine is having not so good of a week.
- On Monday she's sent to the principal's office for cutting off Margaret's hair.
- Tuesday, Margaret's mother is mad at her.
- Wednesday, she's sent to the principal . . . again.
- Thursday, Margaret stops speaking to her.
- Friday starts with yucky eggs and gets worse.
- And by Saturday, even her mother is mad at her.

Okay, fine. Clementine is having a DISASTROUS week.

A 2007 *Boston Globe/Horn Book* Honor Book

★"Humorous scenarios tumble together, blending picturesque dialogue with a fresh perspective as only the unique Clementine can offer. . . . Frazee's engaging pen-and-ink drawings capture the energy and fresh-faced expressions of the irrepressible heroine. . . . A delightful addition to any beginning chapter-book collection."　　　　　—*School Library Journal* (starred review)

The Talented
Clementine

Winner or washout?

When it comes to tackling third grade, Clementine is at the top of her game—okay, so maybe not *all* the time. After her teacher announces that the third and fourth graders will be putting on a talent show, Clementine panics. She doesn't sing or dance or play an instrument. She can't even *hop* with finesse. And as if she didn't feel bad enough, her perfect best friend, Margaret, has so many talents she has to alphabetize them to keep them straight.

As the night of the big "Talent-palooza" draws closer, Clementine is desperate for an act, *any* act. But the unexpected talent she demonstrates at the show surprises everyone—most of all herself.

This *Clementine* sequel is sure to bring the house down!

★"Clementine is a true original, an empathetic human being with the observant eye of a real artist and a quirky, matter-of-fact way of expressing herself. Frazee's line drawings are plentiful and just right. . . . Early chapter-book readers will jump at the chance to spend another eventful week with Clementine."
—*School Library Journal* (starred review)

Clementine's Letter

Clementine can't believe her ears—her beloved teacher, Mr. D'Matz, might be leaving them for the rest of the year to go on a research trip to Egypt! No other teacher has ever understood her impulsiveness, her itch to draw constantly, or her need to play Beat the Clock when the day feels too long. And in his place, he's left a substitute with a whole new set of rules that Clementine just can't figure out. The only solution, she decides, is to hatch a plan to get Mr. D'Matz back. If it means ruining her teacher's once-in-a-lifetime chance—well, it'll be worth it. Won't it?

★ "Irrepressible and delightful Clementine is back. . . . She shines with a vibrant spirit that can never be completely extinguished, even when she is feeling down. Frazee's pen-and-ink drawings perfectly capture Clementine's personality and her world."   —*School Library Journal* (starred review)

Clementine,
Friend of the Week

It's Clementine's turn to be Friend of the Week! She gets to be line leader, collect the lunch money, and feed the fish. Even better, the other kids will make her a booklet, full of the things they value about having her in the class. After reading her friend Margaret's booklet, Clementine begins to get nervous and a little jealous—she *has* to get a great booklet now. Fortunately, she has a lot of astoundishing ideas for getting the kids to write great stuff about her. Unfortunately, just as she's working on the best one, something terrible happens to her beloved kitten, Moisturizer. Worst of all, exactly when she needs a friend the most, Margaret lets her down.

Or does she . . . ?

★"Pennypacker's writing once again brings creativity, humor, and sensitivity to Clementine and her world. Black-and-white line illustrations grace the book, capturing the child's personality and varied emotions. A must-have. . . . Fans will be in for another fun serving of their favorite girl named after a fruit."
—*School Library Journal* (starred review)

Clementine
and the Family Meeting

Clementine's having a nervous breakdown. The FAMILY MEETING! sign is up in her house, and she just knows she's in trouble for something. Has she been too mean to her little brother? Too sloppy? Eating too much junk food? Try as she might to find out what's on the agenda, her parents won't reveal anything before the meeting. As far as Clementine is concerned, the agenda should be something like: "We're getting a gorilla." But no, it's something entirely different. And different doesn't always mean good!

★"Filled with familiar Clementine charm but, more importantly, a whole lot of heart, too."　　—*Kirkus* (starred review)